# Wealth from the Ground

If you are asked to name something made of metal, you can produce a fairly long list—a car, an airplane, a saucepan—but you probably have little or no idea where these metals come from or how they got into their present form.

In this superbly illustrated book, Walter Shepherd explains about the mining of ores, the smelting of iron, the mixing of metals into bronze and other alloys. He describes some of the many uses of rocks, and the way we obtain petroleum to make gasoline. Finally he speaks of fossils and shows how they have helped men to build up an accurate picture of life many centuries ago.

# Finding Out
## About SCIENCE
### Edited by
# KURT ROWLAND

# WEALTH FROM THE GROUND

By WALTER SHEPHERD

Illustrated by GAYNOR CHAPMAN
and CLIFFORD BAYLY

Golden Press ⊗ New York

THIS EDITION PUBLISHED 1966 BY GOLDEN PRESS, INC., NEW YORK.

Library of Congress Catalog
Card Number 62-9348

# Contents

The earth on which we live is a great ball of rock. You can often see the bare rock itself in cliffs and quarries. Pebbles, stones and boulders are only pieces of rock that have been broken off.

There are many different kinds of rock, some hard and others soft. There are red, yellow, brown, black, white and even green rocks, and some are dull looking while others sparkle like sugar. Their appearance depends partly on how they came to be formed and partly on what they are made of.

Inside the earth it is very hot and sometimes the rocks there get red hot and melt. Then they may cool off and set solid again. Rocks formed in this way are very hard, and when broken, sparkle as the light shines on them. This is because they are made up entirely of *crystals* that formed when the molten rock cooled. A common example is *granite*, which is so hard that it is used for paving blocks, large buildings and monuments. Some of the crystals in granite are quite large and are easily seen when the rock is polished. Some are pink, some white and some black.

All rocks formed by heat in this way are called *igneous* or fire-formed rocks, from the Latin word ignis, meaning fire. Though igneous rocks are generally formed deep underground, they may later be raised by movements in the earth's crust and lie uncovered on the surface. The whole of the Dartmoor highland in southwest England, for example, is one huge block of granite covering about 400 square miles.

A lava flow

Some igneous rocks come right up to the surface in the hot, liquid state, flowing out through a volcano as *lava*. Sometimes the lava is full of bubbles of gas and steam, and then it cools to make a sort of stony "sponge" called pumice. This is the pumice stone you may use to get stains off your hands.

Most of the rocks you see at the seaside or in quarries are made in quite a different way. The rain, snow, frost, wind, the heat of the sun, and the waves of the sea gradually break up old rocks and the pieces are washed away by rivers. This goes on all the time and accounts for the pebbles, sand and mud that you can see in rivers and along the shore. This process is called *erosion*, which means wearing away.

Most erosion is caused by water.

It falls as rain and gets into the cracks in the rocks. On a cold night it freezes, and when water freezes it expands or swells. This splits the cracks open and presently pieces of rock are broken right off.

9

Erosion sometimes shapes the rock in strange ways. The form of the rock on the left was caused by wind erosion; in other words, the wind blew sand and dust against the rock and wore it away over many years. In the bottom picture the water eroded part of the rock and so made a natural bridge. Sometimes a river may cut a very deep valley into the rock, as in the picture on the right.

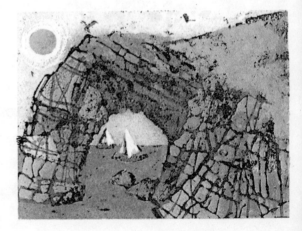

The loosened pieces
of rock tumble downhill
and get carried away by
a stream; and as they are
trundled along they
chip each other's corners
off. Thus they soon
become smooth, round
pebbles and grow
smaller and smaller
all the time.

Presently they form sand grains and if they go on getting smaller still, they eventually make mud.

All this sand and mud finds its way to the bottom of the sea, where it builds up for millions of years, forming layers thousands of feet thick. The weight of the top layers now presses and squeezes the bottom layers into a new kind of hard rock.

It is in this way that sand becomes changed into sandstone, and mud into clay and shale. Even small pebbles may get cemented together to form a kind of natural concrete. This is called "pudding stone" because the pebbles can be seen embedded in it like plums in a pudding.

Solid matter which settles at the bottom of a liquid is called sediment. Rocks formed from sediments that settle on the sea bottom are called *sedimentary rocks*.

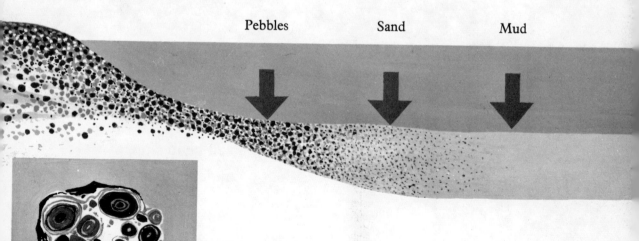

Pebbles     Sand     Mud

Pudding stone

13

Movements of the earth's crust may raise these rocks
above the sea again after many millions of years, and then the
layers can easily be seen in a cliff face. Often they are seen to
have been bent or folded like layers of cloth,

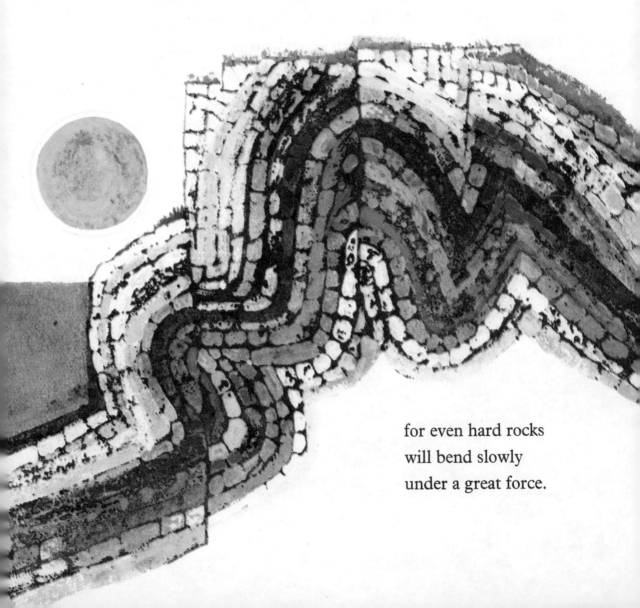

for even hard rocks
will bend slowly
under a great force.

Another kind of rock also forms in the sea. Masses of corals or sea shells collect on the bottom when they die, and are pressed hard to form *limestone*. A very pure, white kind is known as chalk. Limestones make some of the best building stones, and some are roasted to make *lime*, which farmers use to sweeten the soil. Limestone mixed with clay, and then roasted, makes cement.

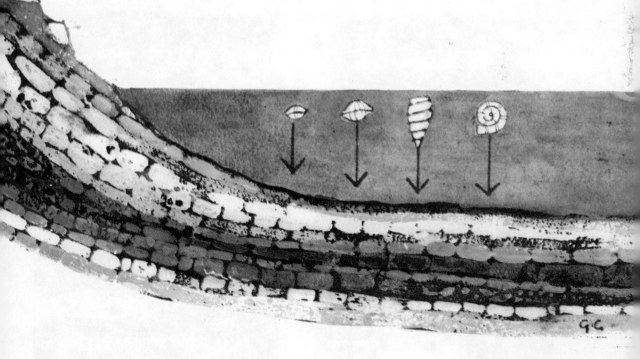

So we have two quite different sorts of rock, igneous and sedimentary. There is still another important group of rocks, but these are made from the other two kinds by a sort of cooking. In the neighborhood of a volcano the heat may gradually change the surrounding rocks, just as the heat of an oven will change a mixture of flour and water into bread.

In this way old igneous rocks may get changed to serpentine, which is often carved into ornaments and polished to show its beautiful green and red streaks. Limestones may be changed to marble.

Other changes may occur under great pressure, and *shales*

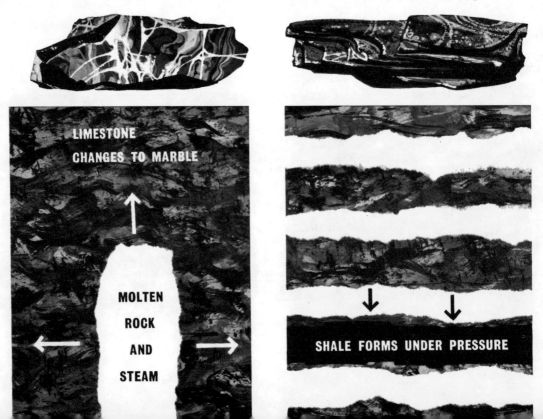

LIMESTONE CHANGES TO MARBLE

MOLTEN ROCK AND STEAM

SHALE FORMS UNDER PRESSURE

are in this way changed to slate, which splits into thin sheets suitable for roofing houses. If heat and pressure occur together, the rocks called schist and gneiss may be formed. All these altered rocks are grouped together under one big name *metamorphic*, which simply means changed in form.

Sedimentary rock                    Igneous rock

From the earliest times man has used the rocks he found in many different ways, for weapons, tools and shelter. To make a knife like the one in this picture took a lot of skill. This period is called the Stone Age.

*Left:* A dagger and arrowhead chipped out of flint 4,000 years ago by a man of the New Stone Age

*Below:* A Stone Age artist's "sketch-book"

Later man learned to put large pieces of stone together to make buildings. Many of these buildings have lasted for hundreds and even thousands of years. Here you can see a house built of granite and another of sandstone, which is a sedimentary rock. You can see that each has a different character.

In many parts of Italy there is a wealth of marble and pieces of different colors are often used together.

Can you think of any other ways in which rocks have been useful to Man? What objects are or have been made of stone?

Rocks are important to Man in other ways too, for they contain minerals. Minerals are the ingredients of which rocks are made just as flour, sugar, butter and eggs are some of the ingredients of which cakes are made. The word *mineral* means something which can be dug out of a mine.

*Above:* A stone-built church,
800 years old

*Right:* A modern steel-frame
and glass building

22

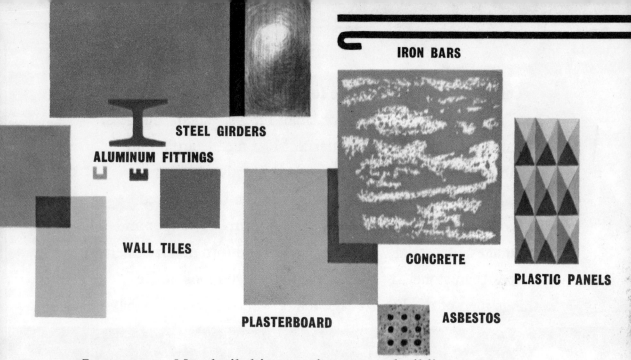

IRON BARS

STEEL GIRDERS

ALUMINUM FITTINGS

WALL TILES

CONCRETE

PLASTIC PANELS

PLASTERBOARD

ASBESTOS

In past ages Man built his most important buildings largely of stone. But a modern building would be impossible without many metals and other minerals as well. If you have ever watched a building such as the one in this picture being constructed you may have noticed steel girders, reinforced concrete, plastic panels, and tiles, aluminum, stainless steel and many other things being used. All these come from minerals, in one way or another. Many more minerals are used which you cannot see; for instance, some of the steel may contain chromium and nickel. More and more different minerals are being used all the time, not only in building but in industry too.

Only a very few metals are found in a pure state. Gold is one; it occurs as tiny grains or small lumps, called "nuggets," in sand, or as fine veins in quartz. Most metals are found combined with other substances in minerals which are called ores, from which the metals have to be separated.

Early man soon discovered that a mixture of copper and tin makes a material which can be worked into much better shapes than stone. It is called bronze. If you look at the things men of the Bronze Age made, you will soon see that it

Copper was probably discovered by accident

was well worth the trouble of mining the ores. Just compare them with the crude objects you saw on pages 18 and 19. A mixture of two or more metals, such as bronze, is called an *alloy*.

A spearhead, axe and shield made 3,000 years ago in the Bronze Age

25

*Right:* Pouring molten steel

*Below:* Kidney ore

Some iron ores are found in very pure masses and can be quarried like rock. One of them is known as "kidney ore" because it looks like a heap of kidneys. Other iron ores are like red or black clay and may form hills or even mountains.

When man found out how to get the iron out of the iron ore he quickly made use of it, as it is a much harder material than bronze. He could make weapons and tools which stood up to a lot more wear and did not have to be repaired as often as bronze. But it took a long time before he was able to *extract* the iron, because the ore has to be mixed with charcoal or coke and heated to a very high temperature in a furnace before the iron will turn liquid and pour out of the ore. This is called *smelting*.

27

*Left:* Works where moist ore is dried before it is taken away to be smelted

The ores of some metals may be found as large crystals in the cracks of rocks through which water has been trickling for thousands or millions of years. As the rain soaks into the ground and runs away through cracks in the rock beneath, it dissolves many of the minerals.

These minerals are scattered about in tiny grains and crystals, much too small to be mined, but the water picks them up and carries them away.

Then a remarkable thing happens. When the water reaches an extra wide crack, or enters a cave where it can partly dry up, it *deposits* or puts down, the minerals that were

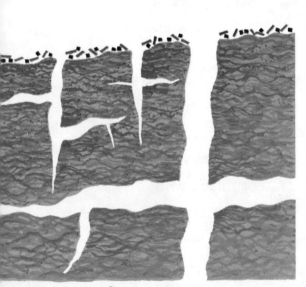

WATER

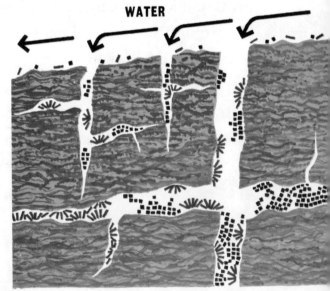

dissolved in it. But it deposits each mineral on top of grains or crystals of the same kind of mineral, so that these begin to grow and become large, pure crystals.

Where there is a tiny crystal of, for instance, silver ore, the water adds more silver ore to it until it becomes a big crystal. It drops its copper on top of more copper ore, and so on, sorting them all out. In this way the water separates the minerals for us in a very convenient way. The cracks in the rocks in which minerals are found are called *veins* or *lodes* by the miners.

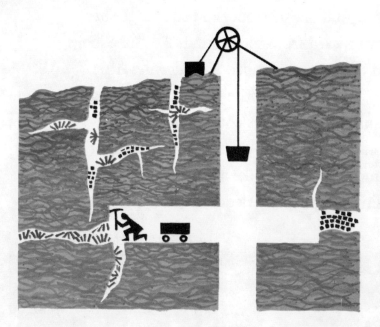

The minerals having been washed out of the rocks by water, and then deposited in cracks as crystals, the miners have sunk a shaft and driven a tunnel to dig them out

29

In districts where the chief rock is limestone, the underground water often washes out large caves or pot holes. The water that drips into these caves contains limestone dissolved in it, and as each drop hesitates before it falls from the roof it dries up very slightly, and leaves a tiny, sparkling crystal of limestone on the roof. The next drop adds another tiny crystal, and so a finger of pure limestone crystals begins to grow downward. It looks like a colored icicle and is called a *stalactite*.

The drops fall from the tip of the stalactite and splash on to the floor of the cave below. Here they dry up a little more and leave another crystal of limestone, and so a finger of crystals also grows upward from the ground. This one looks like a pale colored candle and is called a *stalagmite*. After many thousands of years the stalactite and stalagmite may meet and form a pillar. Some caves contain hundreds of stalactites and look very beautiful when you shine a light on them. They glimmer and sparkle like a grotto in a fairy tale, and you might think you were in Aladdin's cave.

How a stalactite and stalagmite meet each other to form a pillar

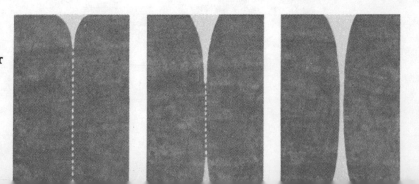

If the water from your faucets comes from a limestone district it contains lime dissolved in it and is said to be "hard". When you boil the water away in a kettle the limestone is deposited on the bottom as "fur". This is the same as stalactite, except that its crystals are too small to sparkle. Large crystals will grow only if the water is *evaporated* very slowly indeed, and a stalactite may take a thousand years to grow an inch long!

The *crystalline* limestone of which stalactites are formed is known as *calcite*, and crystals of it are found filling whole cracks in the rocks. Single crystals may be as clear as glass and measure several inches across, and then they have a very curious effect on light passing through them. If you look through such a crystal you see everything double! The crystal divides each ray of light into two, and the light is said to be *polarized*.

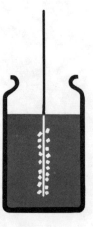

Crystals growing on a piece of string hanging in a strong solution of sugar, as the water slowly evaporates

Rock salt

Each different mineral has its own special form of crystal. Large crystals of calcite called Iceland Spar are generally shaped like a match box that has been pushed slightly out of shape.

Salt is obtained from mines where an old sea has dried up in a desert and become buried. Its natural crystals are perfect cubes. Another crystal that has the form of a cube is fluorspar or "bluejohn," a beautiful rich blue or purple mineral from which ornaments and vases are sometimes made. The gas fluorine, which is used in some rocket propellants, is also obtained from fluorspar. Still another crystalline mineral is selenite or gypsum, and this is mined in large quantities and roasted to make plaster of Paris. This is used, among other things, for facing the ceilings and walls of rooms.

Gypsum

Fluorspar

33

"Smoky" quartz

*Quartz* is a very common mineral that is sometimes deposited by water to form very large crystals indeed. They are shaped like thick pointed rods, each with six sides. When they are colorless they look like glass and are called rock crystal, but sometimes they are stained with delicate colors by traces of metals in them. Manganese gives them a pale purple color and the crystals are then called *amethyst*, iron gives a yellow color and produces *cairngorm*, and so on. Many of

Amethyst

Beryl

these crystals are cut by jewelers and mounted in rings and brooches as semi-precious stones.

The crystals forming very precious stones are made of rarer minerals and some of them, such as beryl, topaz and ruby, contain aluminum. Beryl is deposited by water, but topaz probably arrived in the form of hot vapor.

Emerald            Zircon            Diamond

A diamond is a crystal of pure carbon, the black matter in coal, but it will become a crystal only if it is heated to a very high temperature under enormous pressure. That is why diamonds are found only in rocks that have been buried deep underground.

A sapphire cut as a "brilliant" to make it sparkle

Coal consists of fairly pure carbon and is all that remains of great forests that grew around the mouths of rivers many millions of years ago. The trees lived and died and their leaves and trunks fell into the mud. After many thousands of years a thick layer of them lay buried in the mud. Then the land sank beneath the sea and more sand and mud settled on top of them. These hardened into sedimentary rocks, and their weight squeezed the layer of dead trees into a hard black rock.

A fossil leaf on a piece of shale from a coal mine

Besides the solid minerals which form rocks, like coal and limestone, mineral liquids and gases are also found in some places. Most important of these is *mineral oil*, or petroleum, of which great underground deposits are found in parts of the world. Nobody knows how petroleum was formed, but it is believed to be all that remains of dead forests of seaweed, or perhaps of dead sea creatures.

It is trapped underground by thick layers of rock which cover it like a lid. When holes or wells are bored through this rocky cover, the oil gushes up and is led away through pipes.

Two oil wells, their pipes reaching right down to the store of oil far below

37

Boring holes through the rock, which may be half a mile
thick, is a laborious and expensive job. Sometimes the rock
is so hard that the drills have to be tipped with diamonds
before they will cut it. It may take several months or even
years to drill a deep well, but the petroleum is so valuable
that engineers will sink wells even in the bed of the sea.

You may wonder how they know where to bore such deep
holes. They have several ways of finding out what lies deep
under the ground, and one of them is to explode a small
charge of dynamite just below the surface. The sound of the

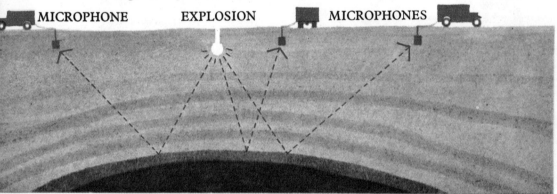

MICROPHONE     EXPLOSION     MICROPHONES

explosion travels down through the rocks, and if there is a
hidden layer of petroleum the sound is reflected back from
its rocky cover. The engineers listen for the echo with sensitive
microphones and can tell how deep it is from the time
taken for the echo to arrive.

38

When the petroleum has been got to the surface it is taken to a refinery, usually through a long pipeline, but sometimes in a special ship called a *tanker*.

When the oil comes out of the ground it is not yet what we call gasoline. It contains many other ingredients as well which have to be separated. This is done at the *refinery*, where the crude oil, as it is called when it leaves the ground, is heated and the vapor allowed to rise inside a tall tower. The drawing at the bottom shows you how the various kinds of oil are removed one by one.

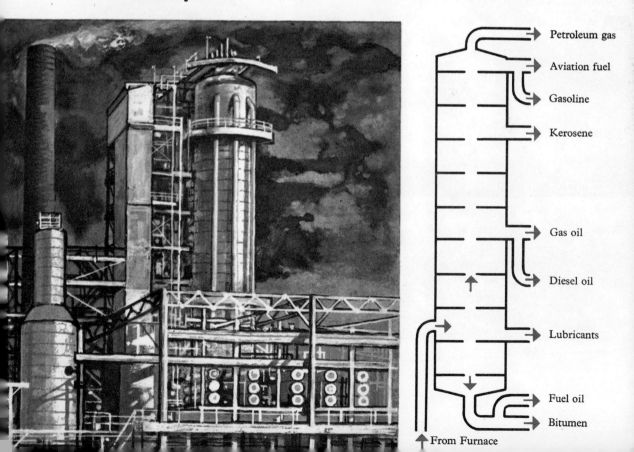

Petroleum gas

Aviation fuel

Gasoline

Kerosene

Gas oil

Diesel oil

Lubricants

Fuel oil

Bitumen

From Furnace

Have you ever seen a piece of amber with an insect trapped inside? Amber is really resin or gum from *prehistoric* pine trees set hard, and when an insect is caught in it, it is perfectly preserved. The insect you can see in this picture is probably 10,000,000 years old.

*Above:* An ammonite

*Left:* A piece of limestone made almost entirely of fossil ammonites

You saw on page 13 how sediments are collecting at the bottom of the sea. While this is going on, creatures are living and dying on the sea floor and their shells and skeletons become buried. Millions of years later when the rocks have been raised and become dry land, quarry workers and miners sometimes break open a rock and find an old shell or skeleton inside it. This has become changed into a kind of stone by the action of water and is called a *fossil*, which means something that has been dug up.

*Above:* A fossil fish 100 million years old

*Left:* Fossilized footprints of an extinct reptile that lived 200 million years ago

41

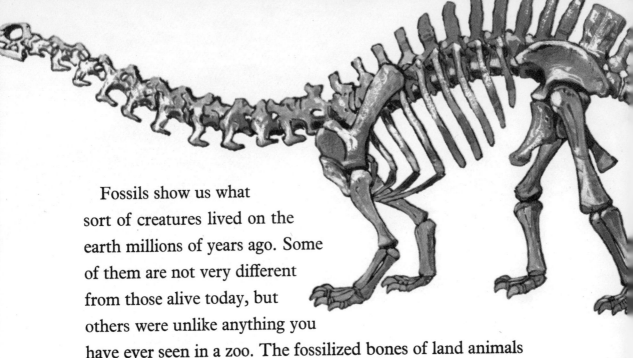

Fossils show us what sort of creatures lived on the earth millions of years ago. Some of them are not very different from those alive today, but others were unlike anything you have ever seen in a zoo. The fossilized bones of land animals are rare. They are found in rocks that were once marshes or river beds, in which the animals were accidentally drowned.

Bones have been found that must have belonged to creatures standing as high as a house, and others to creatures which were covered with thick armor plate to protect them from their enemies. Many of them were like giant crocodiles and some would remind you of the dragons in a fairy story, but none of these monsters is alive today. They have all died out, or become *extinct*.

Often only a few of the bones belonging to an animal can be found, but, in spite of this, scientists can work out what the

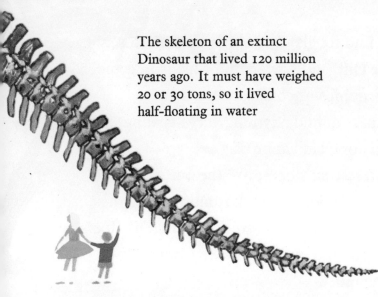

The skeleton of an extinct Dinosaur that lived 120 million years ago. It must have weighed 20 or 30 tons, so it lived half-floating in water

animal was like. Plant fossils— you saw one on page 36—tell them something about the countryside. In this way they are able to build up a picture of what life was like millions of years ago. You must remember that no man ever saw these strange-looking animals and plants. They had gone long before the first man appeared in the world, and that is why they are called prehistoric, which means before the beginning of human history.

You may sometimes find fossils yourself if you look closely at the rocks in a seaside cliff, and you are most likely to come across fossil shells, sea urchins or corals.

But you must not expect to find anything very startling, like the bones of large prehistoric land animals.

You may also find interesting stones, like the one in this picture, with veins of another kind of rock running through them. You will notice that, as the rocks are of different hardness, the softer rock was eroded more quickly, leaving ridges of the harder rock standing out.

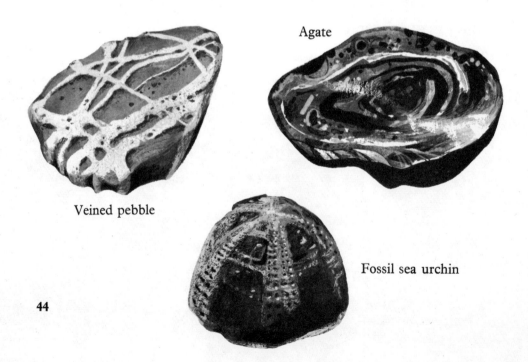

Agate

Veined pebble

Fossil sea urchin

If you wish to understand the countryside in your area, you should visit a local museum. There you will probably be able to see examples of the rocks and minerals which are to be found in your neighborhood. You may also find maps and charts to explain what they are made of and how the countryside came to have its present character.

Throughout this book you have been reading how important minerals have always been to man. Many wars have been fought over the possession of mineral deposits.

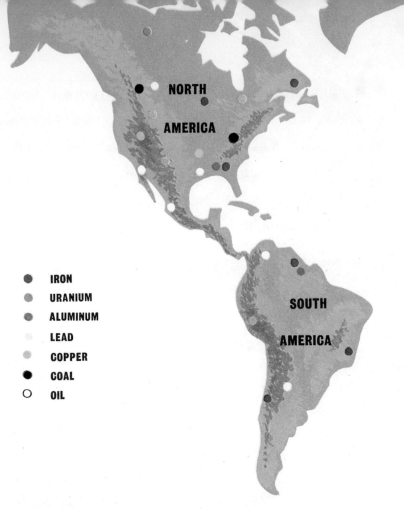

IRON
URANIUM
ALUMINUM
LEAD
COPPER
COAL
OIL

More minerals than ever are needed now and no country has all the minerals it requires. This map shows how the most important minerals are spread throughout the world.

Have you ever wondered what we shall do when the Earth's mineral wealth has run out? We need not be afraid of that, for long before the minerals we use now have given out

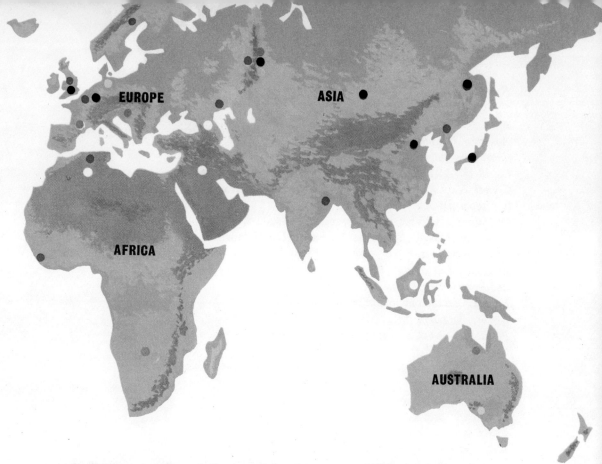

we shall have replaced them with new ones. This is going on all the time. For instance, titanium and aluminum alloys are, for some jobs, taking the place of steel. In power stations coal is turned into electricity, but as more nuclear power stations are built, coal will be replaced by the metal uranium, which is obtained chiefly from the minerals pitchblende and carnotite. When there is no more coal left, we shall probably be in the happy position of not needing any.

*Some of the new words which you read in this book:*

*Alloy.* A mixture of two or more metals
*Amethyst.* Purple-stained quartz
*Cairngorm.* Yellow-stained quartz
*Calcite* (KAL site). Crystalline carbonate of the metal calcium
*Crystal.* A natural piece of any pure substance that always takes the same shape when it is deposited
*Crystalline* (KRIS ta lin). Like a crystal, or made of crystals
*Deposit* (de POZ it). Solids that have settled down in water, or crystals left behind when water has dried up
*Erosion* (ee RO zhun). The wearing away of rocks by the weather, etc.
*Evaporate* (ee VAP o rate). Dry up
*Extinct.* Of a kind no longer living
*Extract.* To take out, or obtain from
*Fossil.* Remains of a plant or animal changed to stone
*Granite* (GRAN it). A hard, sparkling, igneous rock
*Igneous* (IG nee us) *rock.* Rock that has cooled from the molten state
*Lava* (LAH va). Igneous rock that has cooled on the surface of the earth
*Lime.* Oxide of the metal calcium
*Limestone.* Carbonate of calcium, often in the form of shells
*Lode.* A wide vein or network of veins
*Metamorphic rock.* Any rock changed by heat or pressure
*Mineral* (MIN e ral). Any pure substance dug from a mine or quarry or found in rocks
*Mineral oil.* Petroleum as it comes from the ground
*Polarize.* To separate a ray of light into two distinct rays
*Prehistoric* (PREE hiss TOR ic). Before history began
*Quartz.* "Rock crystal," a mineral that looks like glass
*Refinery* (re FINE e ree). A factory where substances are purified
*Sedimentary* (SED i MEN ta ree) *rock.* Any rock formed under water
*Shale.* Clay which splits easily into thin sheets
*Smelting.* Extracting a metal from its ore by heat
*Stalactite* (sta LAK tite). A hanging deposit of crystals of lime like a stone icicle
*Stalagmite* (sta LAG mite). A deposit of crystals of lime on the floor of a cave
*Tanker.* A ship containing large tanks for carrying oil
*Vein* (VANE). A crack in the rocks filled with minerals